Newbridge Discovery Links®

Wolves

Christine Economos

Newbridge

A Haights Cross Communications ◄ Company

Wolves
ISBN: 1-58273-724-X

Program Author: Dr. Brenda Parkes
Content Reviewer: Bruce Hampton, wildlife biologist, Lander, WY
Teacher Reviewer: Lisa Donmoyer, Talbot County Schools, Easton, MD

Written by Christine Economos
Editorial and Design Assistance by Curriculum Concepts

Newbridge Educational Publishing
333 East 38th Street, New York, NY 10016
www.newbridgeonline.com

Copyright © 2002 Newbridge Educational Publishing,
a Haights Cross Communications Company

Cover Photograph: A gray wolf out in the snow
Table of Contents Photograph: Body language suggests this wolf may be in a playful mood.

Photo Credits
Cover: Jeff Lepore/Photo Researchers, Inc.; Contents page: Stephen J. Krasemann/DRK Photo; pages 4–5:
Jim Brandenburg/Minden Pictures; page 6: de Grummond Children's Literature Collection, The University
of Southern Mississippi; page 7: Jeff Lepore/Photo Researchers, Inc.; pages 8–9: Layne Kennedy/CORBIS;
page 10: Jim Brandenburg/Minden Pictures; page 11: Jeff Lapore/Photo Researchers, Inc.; pages 12–13: Jim
Brandenburg/Minden Pictures; page 14: Tim Fitzharris/Minden Pictures; page 16: Jeff Lepore/Photo
Researchers, Inc.; pages 16–17: Layne Kennedy/CORBIS; pages 18–19: Stephen J. Krasemann/DRK
Photo; pages 20–21: Art Wolfe/Photo Researchers, Inc.; pages 22–23: Harvey Lloyd/Peter Arnold, Inc.;
page 24: Jim Brandenburg/Minden Pictures; page 25: William Campbell/Peter Arnold, Inc.; pages 26–27:
Jim Brandenburg/Minden Pictures; page 28: David Northcott/DRK Photo; page 29: (top) Michio
Hoshino/Minden Pictures, (center) Stephen J. Krasemann/DRK Photo, (bottom) Stephen J.
Krasemann/DRK Photo; page 30: Stephen J. Krasemann/DRK Photo

10 9 8 7 6 5 4 3 2

TABLE OF CONTENTS

The Truth About Wolves

On a warm September evening, a lone wolf moves quietly through the forest. It hears a chorus of howls—the pack calling. The wolf answers with a howl of its own. Then it takes off running. In a few minutes, it will join the rest of its pack, and the hunt will continue.

At one time, gray wolves roamed freely throughout North America. But as more and more towns and cities began to replace forests, the wolves' habitat became smaller and smaller. Their populations became so low that they were considered to be **endangered** animals, close to dying off altogether.

Great efforts are being made to save these wolves from extinction and to educate people about these beautiful, yet highly misunderstood, animals.

Even though this nimble hunter is called a gray wolf, its fur can be gray, white, brown, or black.

Many people have gotten the wrong idea about wolves from stories they have read. In folktales, wolves are shown as evil, tricky villains who prey on children. But unlike the wolves in folktales, real wolves are shy and stay away from people. There are no known cases of a healthy, wild wolf ever attacking a human in North America.

Folktales hardly ever show the wolves' beauty and strength. Wolves are **carnivores**, or meat eaters, that are well built for hunting. Their excellent sense of smell helps them to find food in the wild.

Classic folktales such as "Little Red Riding Hood" portray the wolf in a negative way.

You may not think of wolves as dogs, but they are very close relatives. Wolves are the largest members of the canine family.

Their long, strong legs and wide paws enable them to run very fast. Their long, sharp teeth help them to catch, hold on to, and eat prey.

But wolves are more than hunters. They are also loyal and affectionate. To appreciate the truth about wolves, it is important to understand how they live in family units called packs.

A Wolf Family

Wolf packs usually have between six and eight wolves, but some packs have as many as 30. The pack is a very tightly knit family group.

Wolf packs have one male and one female who are the leaders. They are known as the **alpha** male and female. These two wolves rule the pack and keep order. This is important to the pack's survival. In order to hunt successfully and survive, wolves must work together. Fights among wolves only weaken the pack.

Each pack has its own territory that it protects from other wolves. Members of the pack spray their **scent** on trees and bushes around the edges of and within their territory so that other wolves know to keep away. Members of the pack travel and hunt together. They protect their territory and raise their young pups together.

Wolves enjoy the company of other pack members and show one another affection.

While there may be many male and female wolves within a pack, only the alpha male and his female mate have pups. When the pups are born, they are cared for by the alpha male and female. Later, the entire pack cares for them.

In the spring, the alpha female creates a den. Here she will give birth to her pups. When they are born, they are blind and deaf, and have very little fur. They need to stay close to their mother to keep warm.

There are usually five or six pups in a litter. When they are born, the pups weigh only about a pound.

This hungry young pup is licking the mouth of the adult wolf, asking to be fed.

The pups nurse on their mother's milk during the first month. When the pups are two weeks old, their eyes open. At three weeks old, they begin to hear, stand, and walk. They also leave the den and meet the rest of the pack for the first time.

The entire pack looks after the pups. They protect them from hawks, eagles, or other predators that might attack them. They feed the little pups by **regurgitating** food—or bringing it up from their stomachs.

These pups play while the older members of the pack are out hunting.

Since wolves are fierce hunters, sometimes this fierceness carries over into pack life. Wolves may snarl or fight with each other. Fighting can be upsetting to all the wolves in a pack. However, playing helps to relieve tension for both the pups and the adults. It also keeps the wolves friendly with one another and **reinforces** the bonds within a pack.

Pups often roll and tumble in the grass, playfully biting each other. They might hide behind a bush, run and pounce on each other, and wrestle on the ground. That is how pups play, but they are also learning to stalk, chase, and bite—important skills that they will need in order to become hunters. When the pups play, not only are they practicing hunting skills, they also are learning some of the many ways in which wolves communicate with one another.

Howls, Growls, and Wagging Tails

Wolves communicate to show affection, to warn of danger, to keep other wolves out of their territory, and to signal when a hunt will begin.

One way wolves communicate is through **vocalization**, such as howls, barks, snarls, and whimpers. Wolves whimper and whine when they greet one another, and want to show friendliness. When a wolf growls or snarls, it is showing that it is angry.

Each wolf has its own distinct howl. When it is separated from the pack, a wolf will howl to find the pack. Sometimes a pack of wolves will howl together to announce their presence and warn other wolf packs to stay away from their territory.

Of all the vocalizations wolves make, the howl is the only one that can be heard over great distances—up to ten miles away.

In addition to vocalizations, a wolf uses its entire body to communicate. It uses its **stance**, facial expressions, eyes, and even its tail. When a wolf is happy to see another pack member or wants to play, it will often run to the other wolf, bouncing from side to side. A high, wagging tail means the wolf is in a playful mood.

One way that a wolf shows that it is angry is by growling, snarling, and baring its teeth. An angry wolf also will crouch down low with its tail straight out when it is ready to attack.

The alpha wolf uses body language to keep the other wolves in line. Sometimes it will stand on its hind legs to show that it is the boss. Other times the alpha wolf simply stares at an offending wolf. The offending wolf will use body language that communicates surrender

How might other wolves respond to this wolf's expression?

What do you think caused one wolf to crouch down?

or **submission**. A wolf bowing down with its tail between its legs is showing submission.

Good communication helps the pack to cooperate and follow the will of its leaders. Getting along and working well together are essential, especially during a hunt.

Hunters and
Their Prey

Wolves usually hunt large, hoofed mammals, such as deer, elk, caribou, and moose. Because these animals are much larger than they are, the wolves hunt in groups. As a group, the wolves have more strength, and their chances of catching prey are increased.

During the summer, a hunt usually begins at nightfall and can last until morning. One wolf is left behind to be a "pup-sitter" and care for the pups. The rest of the pack heads off to hunt.

The first task for the wolf pack is to find prey. The pack, often led by the alpha female, moves quietly through the forest. The wolves keep their noses to the ground or raised in the air, trying to scent their prey. When they do pick up the scent, they move as a group toward the animal. They must move quickly and quietly. If the animal senses that wolves are close by, it will run away.

This is a bull caribou, a favorite prey for wolves.

When they find their prey, the wolves chase it down. During a chase, the wolves can run as fast as 40 miles per hour. If the animal is part of a herd, the wolves will try to separate it from the herd. Then they surround it. They attack, biting the animal's back, neck, and sides. It would seem that their prey does not have a chance.

But often the hunt is unsuccessful. The prey may pick up the scent of the wolves and run. If the prey is a large moose, it may fight off the wolves. If the wolves feel they cannot win, they give up and continue to look for easy prey, such as old, sick, or very young animals that cannot fight back.

After the wolves have killed an animal, the alpha male and female usually eat before the rest of the pack. When they return to the pups, the adult wolves will regurgitate food for the pups and the "sitter," who has stayed behind.

A wolf pack can stay strong as long as it finds enough meat. But what happens to wolves when there are too few forests to roam through? What happens when there are not enough elk, moose, or other **game** for wolves to hunt?

Wolves can go without food for as long as two weeks. When they do eat, however, they make up for the long period without food. A wolf can eat as much as 20 pounds of meat at one time.

An Uncertain Future

Wolves survive best in unsettled areas, where they can roam and kill wild game. But more and more people are building and settling in places that were once wild. This means that there is less grazing land to feed the elk, moose, caribou, and deer which are the wolves' main food.

In addition, ranchers have struggled for more than a century to coexist with wolves. Hungry wolves sometimes kill and eat livestock such as sheep or cattle. Some ranchers shoot wolves to stop this killing. Hunters also may shoot wolves because the wolves attack game that they themselves are after.

These are some of the reasons why wolves have declined in numbers. About 50 years ago, in most of the United States, except Alaska, wolves had almost disappeared. To some people, this was good news. But in recent years, people have come to realize that an uncertain future for wolves means an uncertain future for many other animals as well.

Wolves can travel as far as 125 miles a day looking for food. But as more and more wild land is cut down to make way for homes and businesses, wolves have less and less hunting area in which to roam.

A herd of elk looks for food in Yellowstone during the winter.

Some of the other animals affected were the large herd animals such as elk, deer, and bison that live in Yellowstone National Park. Long ago, the old and sick herd animals would have been preyed upon by wolves. But during the last 50 years, there have been no wolves around. The herds' weaker animals hung on, eating some of the vegetation that would otherwise have gone to the younger and healthier animals. During severe winters when there was little to eat, thousands of elk, deer, and bison died of starvation.

Park officials decided to bring wolves back to Yellowstone. They hoped the wolves would once again thin out the herds by hunting the old and sick members. Then healthy elk, deer, and bison would have a better chance of finding enough food to survive during the winter.

In 1995, a program was started to reintroduce wolves to Yellowstone Park and wilderness areas in Idaho. Thirty-one wolves were captured in western Canada. Fourteen of them were brought to the park. At first, the wolves were kept in fenced-in areas, but the gates were always kept open. The wolves were free to explore their new surroundings.

Biologists made sure that the wolves they captured were healthy. They checked them for any signs of illness or injury.

Normally, a wolf will try to return to its own territory, where it knows it will be safe. But the wolves in Yellowstone had become familiar with the area before they were released, so they didn't try to find their way back to Canada. They settled in the northern part of Yellowstone where there are thousands of elk, bison, and deer. The wolves have adjusted well to their new environment. They have bred in the wild and had pups. They are also staying in wilderness areas of the national park, and away from human populations.

After six years, park rangers have noticed significant changes in the park's **ecosystem** because of the wolves' reintroduction.

Not everyone is happy with the wolves' reintroduction. Wolves have settled all over the park and in the surrounding wilderness. Ranchers near the park worry that wolves will kill their livestock. If a wolf does attack any livestock, biologists move it to another area.

How Wolves Have Changed the Ecosystem in Yellowstone National Park

Several animal populations in the park have begun increasing since the wolves have been reintroduced. Wolves kill large animals and leave their carcasses. In doing so, they provide food for other animals. With more food available, the numbers of some of these other animals have increased. Another way that wolves have led to an increase in some animal populations has been by killing some of their predators. The comeback of the wolf population has created a healthier ecosystem.

EAGLE

The number of eagles and other scavengers such as wolverines and magpies is increasing because they eat the remains of the carcasses left behind by wolves. More of these animals means a healthier ecosystem.

GRIZZLY BEAR

Grizzly bear populations, once nearly depleted in Yellowstone, are now at healthy numbers. The carcasses that wolves leave behind provide an abundant supply of food for grizzly bears.

WEASEL

Wolves are also preying on coyotes. When there were no wolves in Yellowstone, coyotes increased in large numbers. The coyotes preyed upon small animals such as weasels and foxes, greatly reducing their populations. Now, with the coyote population in check, the numbers of these smaller animals are believed to be increasing.

Wolves are beautiful, intelligent, wild animals as well as skilled hunters. But we now know that when their populations are carefully controlled, they are not destructive. Instead, as has been seen in Yellowstone, wolves play an important role in keeping wilderness areas healthy.

Today, wolves can only survive with people's continued help and understanding. The more we learn about wolves, the closer we will come to finding a way to share this planet with them and with other wild species.

GLOSSARY

alpha: leader of a group of animals

carnivores: animals that eat only meat

ecosystem: an entire area's plants and animals, and how they affect each other and function as a whole unit

endangered: a species or kind of animal threatened with extinction

game: wild animals hunted for food or sport

regurgitating: bringing up food that is not completely digested in order to feed another animal, usually a baby

reinforces: makes stronger

scent: an odor that an animal uses to mark its territory; to smell the odor of an animal

stance: the way an animal or person holds its body; posture

submission: giving in to, or surrendering to another

vocalization: using the voice to make different sounds

WEBSITES

Find out more about wolves at the following:

www.thewildones.org/Animals/graywolf.html

www.yellowstone-natl-park.com/wolf.htm

INDEX